AMAZING ANIMALS
OF THE WORLD ③

Volume 10

Tunicate, Light-Bulb — Zebra, Grevy's

GROLIER
an imprint of
SCHOLASTIC
Scholastic Library Publishing
www.scholastic.com/librarypublishing

First published 2006 by Grolier, an imprint of Scholastic Library Publishing

For information address the publisher: Grolier, Scholastic Library Publishing
90 Old Sherman Turnpike
Danbury, CT 06816

10 digit: Set ISBN: 0-7172-6179–4; Volume ISBN: 0-7172-6189–1
13 digit: Set ISBN: 978-0-7172-6179–6; Volume ISBN: 978-0-7172-6189–5

Printed and bound in the U.S.A.

Library of Congress Cataloging-in-Publications Data:
Amazing animals of the world 3.
p.cm.
Includes indexes.
Contents: v. 1. Abalone, Black–Butterfly, Giant Swallowtail -- v. 2. Butterfly, Indian Leaf–Dormouse, Garden -- v. 3. Duck, Ferruginous–Glassfish, Indian -- v. 4. Glider, Sugar–Isopod, Freshwater -- v. 5. Jackal, Side-Striped–Margay -- v. 6. Markhor–Peccary, Collared -- v. 7. Pelican, Brown–Salamander, Spotted -- v. 8. Salamander, Two Lined–Spider, Barrel -- v. 9. Spider, Common House–Tuna, Albacore -- v. 10. Tunicate, Light-Bulb–Zebra, Grevy's.
ISBN 0–7172–6179–4 (set : alk. paper) -- ISBN 0–7172–6180–8 (v. 1 : alk. paper) -- ISBN 0-7172-6181–6 (v. 2 : alk. paper) -- ISBN 0-7172-6182–4 (v. 3 : alk. paper) -- ISBN 0-7172-6183–2 (v. 4 : alk. paper) -- ISBN 0-7172-6184–0 (v. 5 : alk. paper) -- ISBN 0-7172-6185–9 (v. 6 : alk. paper) -- ISBN 0-7172-6186–7 (v. 7 : alk. paper) -- ISBN 0-7172-6187–5 (v. 8 : alk. paper) -- ISBN 0-7172-6188–3 (v. 9 : alk. paper) -- ISBN 0-7172-6189–1 (v. 10 : alk.paper)
1. Animals--Juvenile literature. I. Grolier (Firm) II. Title: Amazing animals of the world three.
QL49.A455 2006
590—dc22

2006010870

About This Set

Amazing Animals of the World 3 brings you pictures of 400 exciting creatures, and important information about how and where they live.

Each page shows just one species, or individual type, of animal. They all fall into seven main categories, or groups, of animals (classes and phylums scientifically) identified on each page with an icon (picture)—amphibians, arthropods, birds, fish, mammals, other invertebrates, and reptiles. Short explanations of what these group names mean, and other terms used commonly in the set, appear on page 4 in the Glossary.

Scientists use all kinds of groupings to help them sort out the types of animals that exist today and once wandered the earth (extinct species). *Kingdoms*, *classes*, *phylums*, *genus*, and *species* are among the key words here that are also explained in the Glossary.

Where animals live is important to know as well. Each of the species in this set lives in a particular place in the world, which you can see outlined on the map on each page. And in those places, the animals tend to favor a particular habitat—an environment the animal finds suitable for life—with food, shelter, and safety from predators that might eat it. There they also find ways to coexist with other animals in the area that might eat somewhat different food, use different homes, and so on.

Each of the main habitats is named on the page and given an icon, or picture, to help you envision it. The habitat names are further defined in the Glossary on page 4.

As well as being part of groups like species, animals fall into other categories that help us understand their lives or behavior. You will find these categories in the Glossary on page 4, where you will learn about carnivores, herbivores, and other types of animals.

And there is more information you might want about an animal—its size, diet, where it lives, and how it carries on its species—the way it creates its young. All these facts and more appear in the data boxes at the top of each page.

Finally, the set is arranged alphabetically by the most common name of the species. That puts most beetles, for example, together in a group so you can compare them easily.

But some animals' names are not so common, and they don't appear near others like them. For instance, the chamois is a kind of goat or antelope. To find animals that are similar—or to locate any species—look in the Index at the end of each book in the set (pages 45–48). It lists all animals by their various names (you will find the Giant South American River Turtle under Turtle, Giant South American River, and also under its other name—Arrau). And you will find all birds, fish, and so on gathered under their broader groupings.

Similarly, smaller like groups appear in the Set Index as well—butterflies include swallowtails and blues, for example.

Table of Contents
Volume 10

Glossary

Amphibians—species usually born from eggs in water or wet places, which change (metamorphose) into land animals. Frogs and salamanders are typical. They breathe through their skin mainly and have no scales.

Arctic and Antarctic—icy, cold, dry areas at the ends of the globe that lack trees but see small plants grown in thawed areas (tundra). Penguins and seals are common inhabitants.

Arthropods—animals with segmented bodies, hard outer skin, and jointed legs, such as spiders and crabs.

Birds—born from eggs, these creatures have wings and often can fly. Eagles, pigeons, and penguins are all birds, though penguins cannot fly through the air.

Carnivores—they are animals that eat other animals. Many species do eat each other sometimes, and a few eat dead animals. Lions kill their prey and eat it, while vultures clean up dead bodies of animals.

Cities, Towns, and Farms—places where people live and have built or used the land and share it with many species. Sometimes these animals live in human homes or just nearby.

Class—part or division of a phylum.

Deserts—dry, often warm areas where animals often are more active on cooler nights or near water sources. Owls, scorpions, and jack rabbits are common in American deserts.

Endangered—some animals in this set are marked as endangered because it is possible they will become extinct soon.

Extinct—these species have died out altogether for whatever reason.

Family—part of an order.

Fish—water animals (aquatic) that typically are born from eggs and breathe through gills. Trout and eels are fish, though whales and dolphins are not (they are mammals).

Forests and Mountains—places where evergreen (coniferous) and leaf-shedding (deciduous) trees are common, or that rise in elevation to make cool, separate habitats. Rain forests are different. (see Rain forests)

Fresh Water—lakes, rivers, and the like carry fresh water (unlike Oceans and Shores, where the water is salty). Fish and birds abound, as do insects, frogs, and mammals.

Genus—part of a family.

Grasslands—habitats with few trees and light rainfall. Grasslands often lie between forests and deserts, and they are home to birds, coyotes, antelope, and snakes, as well as many other kinds of animals.

Herbivores—these animals eat mainly plants. Typically they are hoofed animals (ungulates) that are common on grasslands, such as antelope or deer. Domestic (nonwild) ones are cows and horses.

Hibernators—species that live in harsh areas with very cold winters slow down their functions then and sort of sleep through the hard times.

Invertebrates—animals that lack backbones or internal skeletons. Many, such as insects and shrimp, have hard outer coverings. Clams and worms are also invertebrates.

Kingdom—the largest division of species. Commonly there are understood to be five kingdoms: animals, plants, fungi, protists, and monerans.

Mammals—these creatures usually bear live young and feed them on milk from the mother. A few lay eggs (monotremes like the platypus) or nurse young in a pouch (marsupials like opossums and kangaroos).

Migrators—some species spend different seasons in different places, moving to where more food, warmth, or safety can be found. Birds often do this, sometimes over long distances, but other types of animals also move seasonally, including fish and mammals.

Oceans and Shores—seawater is salty, often deep, and huge. In it live many fish, invertebrates, and even some mammals, such as whales. On the shore, birds and other creatures often gather.

Order—part of a class.

Phylum—part of a kingdom.

Rain forests—here huge trees grow among many other plants helped by the warm, wet environment. Thousands of species of animals also live in these rich habitats.

Reptiles—these species have scales, lungs to breathe, and lay eggs or give birth to live young. Dinosaurs are thought to have been reptiles, while today the class includes turtles, snakes, lizards, and crocodiles.

Scientific name—the genus and species name of a creature in Latin. For instance, Canis lupus is the wolf. Scientific names avoid the confusion possible with common names in any one language or across languages.

Species—a group of the same type of living thing. Part of an order.

Subspecies—a variant but quite similar part of a species.

Territorial—many animals mark out and defend a patch of ground as their home area. Birds and mammals may call quite small or quite large spots their territories.

Vertebrates—animals with backbones and skeletons under their skins

Light-Bulb Tunicate
Clavelina huntsmani

Length: 2 inches
Width: ⅜ inch
Diet: plankton and dissolved organic matter
Methods of Reproduction: budding and egg layer

Home: coastal Pacific Ocean from British Columbia to Southern California
Order: Enterogonid sea squirts
Family: Clavelinid tunicates

 Oceans and Shores

 Other Invertebrates

© BRANDON D. COLE / CORBIS

The light-bulb tunicate is named for its obvious resemblance to an ordinary light bulb. The curved shape of its transparent body is traced by a bright pink or pale yellow line, particularly at the body's narrower end. Tunicates, also called sea squirts, are small, baglike animals that spend their lives attached to rocks and other solid objects on the seafloor. Each individual has two openings, or siphons, in its simple body. Water enters one opening and is pumped out through the other. This flow of water delivers both food and oxygen.

Light-bulb tunicates live in coastal ocean waters. They cluster in colonies that hang from the undersides of rock ledges, or they cling to vertical rock faces. Each colony measures about three inches high and up to 20 inches wide.

Light-bulb tunicates reproduce in one of two ways. A solitary tunicate can produce buds, which grow into exact replicas of itself. In this way a single tunicate can blossom into an entire colony. Individuals already in a colony often produce eggs. The colonial tunicate keeps its eggs near its inhalant siphon, where they receive a fresh supply of oxygen-rich water. The eggs hatch into bright orange embryos, which can be seen through the adult's transparent body. The embryos transform into tadpolelike larvae that the adult spews into the water. Within a day the freed tadpoles mature into adults and begin to form colonies of their own.

Ruddy Turnstone
Arenaria interpres

Length: 9 inches
Wingspan: 17½ inches
Diet: crustaceans, mollusks, and insects
Number of Eggs: 3 to 5

Home: Arctic coastlines of Eurasia and North America
Order: Shorebirds
Family: Turnstones, sandpipers, and plovers

 Arctic and Anarctic

 Birds

© TIM ZUROWSKI / CORBIS

The rocky Arctic coast may not sound like a summer-vacation resort, but it's perfect for the ruddy turnstone. In the spring, these shorebirds begin flying north from warm places like South America and the Gulf of Mexico. After a few rest stops along the Atlantic Ocean and at the Great Lakes, they reach the Arctic in May or early June.

The Arctic shores are well stocked with food for the ruddy turnstone, which gets its name from the unique way it finds food. As it wanders along the shore, it uses its short, slightly upturned bill to overturn stones—as well as shells and clumps of dirt. Then it feasts on the creatures it finds underneath: worms, insects, and small crustaceans.

Sometimes it digs its bill deep into the sand for a snack of crab eggs or snails.

When it's not eating, the ruddy turnstone spends time playing. It seems to enjoy swimming, bathing, and preening itself in the ocean. The bird is also friendly with people and will often take food from their hands.

The female turnstone lays her eggs soon after she arrives in the Arctic. The treeless tundra and rocky coast do not offer much privacy or comfort, so the bird makes only the crudest of nests by scratching out a shallow hole in the ground or placing bits of dried plants in a rocky crevice. The female lays green eggs with black spots, while the male protects her from intruders.

Aldabra Turtle
Geochelone gigantea

Length: 32 to 48 inches
Weight: up to 500 pounds
Diet: green plants and fruits
Method of Reproduction: egg layer

Home: islands of Aldabra, the Seychelles, Mauritius, and Réunion
Order: Turtles and tortoises
Family: Tortoises

 Grasslands

 Reptiles

© JOCHEN TACK / PETER ARNOLD, INC.

The enormous Aldabra turtle looks like the more famous Galápagos tortoise. In fact, these two species are close cousins, the last surviving members of a group of giant, slow-moving, long-lived tortoises. At one time the Aldabra turtle inhabited islands throughout the Indian Ocean. Unfortunately, it has been all but wiped out by humans and domestic animals. The turtle's eggs and young were destroyed by roaming dogs, cats, and pigs. Despite its gigantic size, the adult Aldabra was no match for hunting parties, who could topple the turtle onto its back or shoot it.

One wild population of Aldabra turtles has survived the onslaught of civilization. Some 150,000 individuals live on the four islands of Aldabra. Nearby, on the Seychelle Islands, the government has fenced in its turtles to keep them safe. Aldabra turtles have also been shipped to Mauritius and Réunion islands, and to foreign zoos.

Despite its name, this turtle is a true tortoise, designed for life on dry land. But like turtles, it must drink lots of water. As a result, Aldabras never venture far from fresh water. Like the Galápagos tortoise, the Aldabra has an enormous, highly domed shell, or carapace. An important difference between their shells is the Aldabra's "nuchal scute," a bony plate at the front of the shell. This plate helps protect the tortoise's vulnerable neck.

Alligator Snapping Turtle
Macroclemys temminickii

Length: up to 5 feet
Weight: up to 200 pounds
Diet: fish, reptiles, and
mollusks

Number of Eggs: 8 to 52
Home: southern United States
Order: Tortoises and turtles
Family: Snapping turtles

  Fresh Water

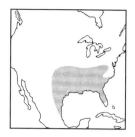

Reptiles

Imagine that you are a hungry fish swimming along the murky bottom of the Mississippi River. You see a delicious-looking red worm squirming about near some rocks. You might think you have found lunch. But if you grab for this worm, it will be you who will be eaten.

What appeared to be a red worm was actually a decoy, a strip of muscle fastened to the tongue of an alligator snapping turtle. This powerful turtle—so strong it can bite off a person's hand—likes to lie on a muddy river bottom, open its mouth, and lure fish to their doom. Alligator snapping turtles spend almost all their time underwater, coming up only for an occasional gulp of air. The only time females leave the water is to lay their eggs in spring. They haul their scary-looking bodies onto the shore, crawl about 450 feet, and dig a funnel-shaped hole. They pause only long enough to deposit their eggs and cover the hole, then immediately return to the water.

When they are born, alligator snapping turtles are small and vulnerable. They may be eaten on their way to the water by large birds or other predatory land animals. Once in the water, they are sometimes eaten by adults of their own species. But an alligator snapping turtle that survives to adulthood has little to fear. This reptile is one of the world's largest freshwater turtles. Its spiked shell and powerful, alligatorlike snout are enough to intimidate most anyone.

Australian Snake-Necked Turtle
Chelodina longicollis

Length: 4 to 10 inches
Diet: insects, tadpoles, frogs, and small fish
Number of Eggs: 10 to 15

Home: southeastern Australia
Order: Turtles and tortoises
Family: Snake-necked turtles

 Fresh Water

 Reptiles

© KLAUS UHLENHUT / ANIMALS ANIMALS / EARTH SCENES

The Australian snake-necked turtle differs from North American and European turtles in a very basic way: it cannot pull its neck and head inside its shell. When attacked, this fascinating turtle must bend its long neck sideways, wrapping it beneath the rim of its shell. A covering of warty skin gives some protection to the vulnerable neck. But the creature's best defense is to make a hasty retreat. As a result, the turtle is always watchful for enemies. At the slightest sign of danger, it dives into water and swims away with great speed. When the turtle is cornered, its final defense is to produce a horrible-smelling white liquid from scent glands. Because of its smell, the Australians have nicknamed this turtle "stinker."

The turtle uses its neck in much the same way that a true snake uses its body: when a small fish or tadpole swims near, the turtle strikes out swiftly. When not hunting, the turtle sunbathes on partially submerged rocks or floating mats of weeds.

The snake-necked turtle is a familiar sight in the rainy regions of southeastern Australia. It seldom wanders far from water, favoring marshes, ponds, and swampy edges of lakes and rivers. November is nesting season, a time when females emerge during strong rainstorms. They remain out of the water just long enough to dig their nests in the muddy soil and deposit their eggs. The orange-spotted hatchlings dig out in spring.

Chinese Softshell Turtle
Trionyx sinensis

Length of the Shell: up to 10 inches
Diet: fish, freshwater crustaceans, and mollusks
Method of Reproduction: egg layer

Home: eastern China, the Koreas, Vietnam, Japan, and Hawaii
Order: Turtles and tortoises
Family: Softshell turtles

 Rain forests

Reptiles

© MICHAEL DICK / ANIMALS ANIMALS / EARTH SCENES

Chinese softshell turtles look quite different from the turtles that are common in North America. They are easily recognized by their shiny, pancake-shaped shell, or carapace. True to their name, their shell is smooth and leathery, unlike the hard and plated shell of their North American cousins. The turtle's legs are flattened like paddles, and its feet are webbed. The softshell uses its long, odd-looking nose as a snorkel, breathing with only its nostrils above the water. These special adaptations make the Chinese softshell turtle a strong, fast swimmer.

Most softshell turtles live in eastern Asia. The Chinese variety is a dark olive-green with black spots. Its carapace is decorated with long rows of small, wartlike bumps. Like most softshells, this species has a long neck and sharp jaws. It can quickly whip its neck from side to side, delivering a sharp bite to anything that disturbs it. Chinese softshells live in slow-moving streams and canals, and in lakes and large pools. They seldom leave the water because they require moisture to survive. The turtle rests during the day and hunts throughout the night. It cruises rapidly across the water bottom, searching for fish and stirring up freshwater mollusks and crustaceans.

In the spring mating season, males fight ferociously over territories and females. After breeding, the female lays her eggs in a hole dug into the bank of a river or lake.

European Pond Turtle
Emys orbicularis

Length of the Carapace: 4½ to 10 inches
Diet: invertebrates, small fish, frogs, and newts
Method of Reproduction: egg layer

Home: Europe, western Asia and North Africa
Order: Turtles
Family: Freshwater and map turtles

 Fresh Water

 Reptiles

© HANS REINHARD / BRUCE COLEMAN INC.

European pond turtles live in ponds, swamps, canals, and slow-moving rivers filled with plants. On hot days the turtles float on the water's surface or crawl onto land to sun themselves. They are shy creatures. At the slightest disturbance, they quickly disappear to the bottom of the water, where they can hide among the plants. European pond turtles have dark upper shells marked with light-green or yellow lines and spots. This coloring camouflages them well, making the creatures all but "invisible" among the plants.

In early morning and in the evening, pond turtles hunt for food. They eat mainly insect larvae, tadpoles, and small fish. Most of the fish they catch are weak or dying. In this way, European pond turtles help to keep their habitat clean.

The turtle's shell is oval and flatter than the shell of a land turtle. This gives pond turtles a more streamlined shape, making it easier for them to swim through the water. The shell has two main parts. The upper part is the carapace; the lower part is the plastron. They are joined on each side by an elastic bridge. The shell protects the turtle's body. The turtle can withdraw its head, limbs, and tail under the carapace for safety.

The European pond turtle lives in a wide range. But its range and its population have decreased because humans are destroying its habitats. People have drained ponds and swamps for farms, houses, and other uses.

Hawksbill Turtle
Eretmochelys imbricata

Length of the Shell: up to 3 feet

Weight: up to 165 pounds

Number of Eggs: 5 nests of 150 eggs each, laid every other year

Diet: sponges, shellfish, and fish

Home: Atlantic, Indian, and Pacific oceans

Order: Turtles

Family: Sea turtles

 Oceans and Shores

 Reptiles

© STUART WESTMORLAND / CORBIS

Endangered Animals

Like other sea turtles, the hawksbill spends most of its life in the water, but crawls onto land to lay eggs. Once she has mated, the female hawksbill turtle searches for a good place to bury her eggs. She may wander hundreds of yards, sniffing the ground carefully, before she chooses just the right spot. She digs a hole 2 or 3 feet wide and 6 to 8 inches deep. After she deposits her eggs, the mother turtle carefully buries them. She then turns and slowly makes her way back to the sea.

Eight to nine weeks later, the eggs hatch. The young hawksbill turtles push away the blanket of sand and head straight for the water. It will take the young turtles three to four years to mature. As they mature, hawksbill turtles learn to eat sponges. They use their sharp, beaklike mouths to scrape the sponges off rocks and coral reefs. As you may have guessed, it is the shape of this turtle's mouth that gives it its name.

The hawksbill turtle is an endangered species. There are very few left, mostly because people have hunted them for thousands of years. The hawksbill's carapace, or shell, is used to make tortoiseshell jewelry, ornaments, and eyeglass frames. The Roman emperor Nero is said to have even had a bathtub made of beautiful hawksbill shells. Fortunately, the nations of the world have now agreed to protect this species.

Kemp's Ridley Sea Turtle
Lepidochelys kempi

Length: about 28 inches
Home: Gulf of Mexico and the western Atlantic Ocean between Nova Scotia and the Bahamas

Diet: crabs, snails, clams, jellyfish, and fish
Number of Eggs: about 100
Order: Turtles and tortoises
Family: Marine turtles

 Oceans and Shores

Reptiles

Endangered Animals

© JEFF SIMON / BRUCE COLEMAN INC.

Each spring, Kemp's ridley turtles perform their annual ritual at an isolated beach along Mexico's Gulf coast. On a windy, rainy day, female ridleys emerge from the surf and lay their golf-ball-sized eggs in the sand. That done, the females return to the sea, leaving behind their offspring to hatch by themselves. About 60 days later, the baby ridleys dig themselves out of their sandy nests and scramble down to the surf. In the 1800s, tens of thousands of ridleys participated in this annual event. Today the number is in the hundreds at best.

Many factors have played into the ridley's plight. At sea, adult ridley sea turtles die in nets and traps meant for fish

and shrimp. On the beach, people have, until recently, dug up the turtle's eggs and sold them at the market. The eggs left behind were preyed upon by coyotes, raccoons, and skunks. The few sea turtles that managed to hatch and make it to the water faced predation, or being eaten, by fish, crabs, and birds.

In recent years, U.S. and Mexican citizens have joined forces to save the ridley. It is now illegal to harvest or sell ridley eggs. Each year, volunteers gather ridley hatchlings and raise them until they are large enough to defend themselves. Some wildlife experts fear that the population of Kemp's ridley turtles is simply too small to ever recover.

Leatherback Turtle
Dermochelys coriacea

Length: 4 to 6 feet
Weight: 650 to 1,200 pounds
Diet: jellyfish, crustaceans, and mollusks
Number of Eggs: 50 to 170

Home: Atlantic, Pacific, and Indian oceans
Order: Turtles and tortoises
Family: Leatherback turtles

 Oceans and Shores

 Reptiles

© FRED BRUEMMER / PETER ARNOLD, INC.

(?)
Endangered Animals

The leatherback turtle is the largest of all the living turtles. It gets its name from the leathery skin that covers its carapace, or shell. An extremely powerful swimmer, this sea turtle travels much farther from the tropics than do other marine turtles. It has been found in both temperate and subarctic waters. The leatherback can live in these cold waters because, unlike most reptiles, it can generate some internal body heat.

The female leatherback turtle leaves the water only to lay her eggs. During her brief visit to land, always a tropical beach, she digs her nest, lays her eggs, then circles the eggs once before returning to the ocean. No one is really sure why she does this—

perhaps to help her remember where the nest is, or to help her find the ocean again. Her newly hatched babies also circle the nest before heading for the water.

The leatherback is in extreme danger of extinction. Although the adult turtle is rarely hunted, its eggs are eaten by many beachcombing animals, including humans. An even greater threat to the leatherback's survival is the development of beach resorts on shores that the turtle needs for nesting. Every year, many of the creatures die after ingesting trash dumped into the ocean. Leatherbacks often mistake plastic bags for jellyfish, their favorite meal. The bags can suffocate the turtles or block their stomachs, causing them to starve to death.

Loggerhead Turtle
Caretta caretta

Length: about 3 feet
Diet: jellyfish, clams, squid, fish, and sea plants
Home: Atlantic Ocean from Maine to Argentina, southern Pacific Ocean

Weight: about 300 pounds
Number of Eggs: 50 to 1,000
Order: Turtles
Family: Hard-backed sea turtles

 Oceans and Shores

 Reptiles

© NORBERT WU / MINDEN PICTURES

Endangered Animals

On a sandy beach during a summer night in Florida or Australia, you may be lucky enough to see dozens of tiny loggerhead turtles burst from the sand and wriggle their way down to the sea. These hatchling sea turtles are taking the first dangerous steps of their lives. Eventually they may grow up to be large, imposing animals. But on this night, they are almost defenseless against predators such as crabs, birds, and sharks. The bite-sized hatchlings must race to deep water or risk being eaten.

If a tiny loggerhead can swim 30 to 50 miles from shore, it will find rafts of floating seaweed in which to hide. Yet only one loggerhead in 1,000 (some say only one in 10,000) survives to return to the beach where it was born—the beach where it will lay its own eggs.

The life of a loggerhead has always been risky. People in many countries eat its eggs, and others make jewelry and combs from its shell. Still more turtles are harmed unintentionally. The lights around resorts and beachside homes confuse emerging hatchlings. At sea, many turtles drown when they get tangled in shrimp nets.

Conservationists have succeeded in getting laws passed that force shrimp fishermen in U.S. waters to put turtle escape doors in their nets. Many Florida cities now ban beach lights at night. And volunteers help disoriented hatchlings find their way back to the beach and into the surf.

Pig-Nosed Softshell (Fly River) Turtle
Carettochelys insculpta

Length of the Shell: up to 20 inches

Number of Eggs: usually 15 to 20

Diet: crustaceans, fish, plants, and fruits

Weight: up to 35 pounds

Home: New Guinea and northern Australia

Order: Turtles and tortoises

Family: Pitted-shell turtles

 Fresh Water

 Reptiles

© TOM MCHUGH / PHOTO RESEARCHERS

The pig-nosed softshell, or Fly River, turtle, is the last surviving member of an ancient family of turtles. Today it is found only in southern New Guinea, in the region of the Fly River, and in the Northern Territory of Australia. Yet 28 million years ago, the turtle's ancestors roamed North America, Europe, and Asia.

This unusual freshwater turtle is similar to sea turtles in that its legs and feet look like flippers. It can use its odd-looking "pig nose" as a snorkel, enabling it to breathe while just under the surface of the water. This turtle is called a "softshell" because its carapace (the top half of its shell) lacks bony plates and is covered with soft skin.

But the turtle differs from true softshells in many ways. For example, its plastron (the underside of the shell, which covers the belly) is bony and rigid. Also, the turtle's shell actually expands slightly with each breath.

During the dry season (September to November), the turtles mate. The female digs a shallow nest in a sandy riverbank. When the young turtles hatch, they are just two inches long.

The native Kiwai people of Papua New Guinea consider the Fly River turtle sacred. In fact, they believe that any man who kills one will lose his ability to father children.

Wood Turtle
Clemmys insculpta

Length: up to 10 inches
Diet: worms, slugs, insects, tadpoles, and fruits
Home: northeastern North America

Number of Eggs: 6 to 8
Order: Turtles and tortoises
Family: Box turtles and water turtles

 Forests and Mountains

 Reptiles

© DAVID A. NORTHCOTT / CORBIS

The handsome wood turtle is a very clever animal. To get to a farmer's field, it patiently searches for a hole in the fence. If there is no hole, this medium-size turtle will start to climb. Reportedly, it can scale a 6-foot-high chain-link fence! The turtle does not eat the farmer's crops; it simply wants the worms that the farmer uncovers with his plow. The turtle even helps the farmer by eating slugs and insect pests.

The wood turtle's rough, sculptured shell, or carapace, is unmistakable. Each section, or scute, of the shell is shaped like a small, uneven pyramid. The top of the turtle's shell is usually dark brown. The portion of the shell that covers the wood turtle's belly—

the plastron—is yellow. The creature is affectionately known as "old redlegs" because of the reddish-orange skin on its front legs and neck.

Wood turtles live in cold woodland streams and marshy meadows. After mating in spring, the female deposits her eggs in a shallow hole. Most hatchlings emerge in fall, but some spend winter in the nest, scrambling out the following spring.

At one time, many people hunted wood turtles for their meat. This is now illegal in several states because the species has become rare. Unfortunately, some people continue to hunt wood turtles illegally and also collect them as pets.

Desert Horned Viper
Cerastes cerastes

Length: 18 to 30 inches
Diet: lizards, mice, and other small rodents
Method of Reproduction: egg layer

Home: northern Africa and southwestern Asia
Order: Lizards and snakes
Family: Vipers

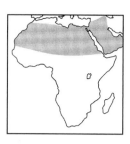

 Deserts

 Reptiles

© DANIEL HEUCLIN / NHPA

To avoid the hot, drying sun, the desert horned viper stays indoors during the day. Its lair can be found deep inside a rocky outcropping, where temperature and humidity stay at bearable levels.

As soon as the sun sets, the viper crawls from its nest and drops to the sand. There it races away like a sidewinder, whipping its body in the shape of an *S*. A desert horned viper ambushes its prey. It approaches through the sand in total silence and then pounces—delivering a venomous bite that stuns its victim.

The desert horned viper eats small animals such as desert pack rats and sand skinks. It seldom attacks large animals or humans. When frightened, a desert horned viper first tries to hide its tan-colored body in the sand. If this does not work, the snake warns its enemy with a loud rasping noise. The horned viper makes this sawlike sound with its heavy, stiff scales. It loops its scaly body over itself and rubs. If this final warning is ignored, the viper will strike.

Horned vipers are named for the hornlike scales above their eyes. These snakes can also be recognized by their huge, triangular head and small eyes. Without large eyes, the snake's night vision would be poor. Scientists believe that the creature tracks its prey by sensing the heat from the victim's body.

Levantine Viper
Vipera lebetina

Length: 2½ to 6 feet
Diet: small mammals, birds, and lizards
Methods of Reproduction: egg layer and live-bearer

Home: northern Africa, Eastern Europe, and western Asia
Order: Lizards and snakes
Family: Vipers and pit vipers

 Grasslands

 Reptiles

© JOHN MITCHELL / PHOTO RESEARCHERS

The venom of the levantine viper is very toxic. This greatly feared snake kills not only humans, but also camels and horses that may accidentally step near it. This is the "cursed viper" often mentioned in biblical stories. The nomadic people of northern Africa and the Middle East also repeat ancient myths about the levantine viper.

Levantine vipers take their name from the "Levant," a region that includes the eastern part of the Mediterranean. In reality, this viper's range extends over a much larger region, from Morocco to Iraq. Within this large range are seven distinct races, or subspecies, of levantine viper. Their appearances and lifestyles differ to accommodate their different habitats.

Levantine vipers also differ in the manner in which they give birth. Generally subspecies living in cool northern countries lay eggs. Those in the south usually give birth to live young.

Throughout their range, levantine vipers live in dry, barren areas, such as brushy hillsides and rocky ravines. They prey on all sorts of small animals and often climb into bushes to catch sleeping birds. When the weather is cool, the viper is active during the day, after warming itself in the morning sun. In hot weather, it hunts at night and spends the day in rock crevices, fallen logs, or abandoned burrows. Some levantine vipers hide in rubbish piles—posing a particular danger to unwary humans and their pets.

Malayan Pit Viper
Calloselasma rhodostoma

Length: 24 to 40 inches
Diet: small mammals, birds, and frogs
Number of Eggs: 12 to 25

Home: southeastern Asia
Order: Lizards and snakes
Family: Vipers and pit vipers

 Rain forests

Reptiles

© DAVID M. DENNIS / ANIMALS ANIMALS / EARTH SCENES

Hikers in the southeastern section of Asia are wise to know the physical characteristics of the venomous Malayan pit viper. Distinguishing features are a large, triangular head and a light stripe that extends from eye to ear. Yet from a few feet away, the viper's dark brown body is well camouflaged in the shady jungle floor. During the day, this snake lies hidden under rocks or in thick weeds. It is most abundant along the forest edge and in tropical plantations. Unfortunately, this is where people are most likely to accidentally step on or otherwise disturb the viper.

The bite of a large Malayan pit viper can be dangerous. As in all vipers, its venom is a mixture of blood poisons. The pit viper injects its poison into a victim through hollow, needlelike teeth in its upper jaw. When the snake opens its mouth to strike, its fangs swing forward. Unless it is directly stepped on, the Malayan pit viper usually warns an intruder before biting by curling up its body and shaking its tail.

When left undisturbed, the Malayan pit viper sleeps until sunset. Then it silently slithers from its nest to hunt until dawn. It can locate warm-blooded prey, such as mice, by means of two heat-sensitive organs, or "pits," on its snout. Among the Malayan pit viper's American cousins are the venomous copperheads and rattlesnakes. Unlike most vipers, this Malaysian species produces eggs rather than live young.

Meadow Viper (Field Adder)
Vipera ursinii

Length: 16 to 20 inches
Diet: locusts, lizards, and mice
Method of Reproduction:
   live-bearer

Home: Eurasia
Order: Lizards and snakes
Family: Vipers

 Grasslands

 Reptiles

© DANIEL HEUCLIN / PETER ARNOLD, INC.

The meadow viper is recognized by the dark, wavy line that runs down its back and tail. The scales of the male are yellowish-brown or olive-green; the female's are mainly brown. Beneath the snake's scales lie dark spots that speckle its grayish skin.

Meadow vipers are known by many names throughout Europe and Asia because they occur in several distinct groups. Some have been separated for so long that they look quite different from one another. For example, the Italian meadow viper (found only in central Italy) measures barely 16 inches, is rather skinny, and has very small eyes. The French meadow viper (found high in the French Alps) has unusually large eyes and is paler in color than the others. The largest and most vividly colored meadow viper is the steppe viper of Romania and southern Russia. Most meadow vipers live high in the mountains and prowl along the edges of wooded areas. The one exception is the Danubian meadow viper, which lives in the damp Danube Valley from Vienna to the Black Sea.

Despite these differences, all meadow vipers are the same species. Individuals from one group, or subspecies, often breed with those in another group. One thing all meadow vipers have in common is their venomous bite. They have hollow fangs with which they inject venom into their prey. Only exceptionally large meadow vipers are dangerous to humans.

Peruvian Mountain Viscacha
Lagidium peruanum

Length of the Body: up to 20 inches
Length of the Tail: up to 15 inches
Diet: grasses, herbs, and lichen

Weight: 2 to 4½ pounds
Number of Young: usually 1
Home: Peru and Bolivia
Order: Rodents
Family: Chinchillas and viscachas

 Forests and Mountains

 Mammals

© DAVID MCNEW / PETER ARNOLD, INC.

The viscacha is closely related to the chinchilla. The viscacha's soft, thick, woolly fur is almost as luxurious as its cousin's costly pelt. There are two main types of viscachas. The plains viscacha lives a nocturnal life on the South American pampas. The mountain viscacha dwells high in the Andes Mountains. It is active during the day, when it searches its craggy habitat for the little food available there. Mountain viscachas are powerful and agile jumpers. Their padded feet enable them to climb straight up steep, rocky cliffs.

Of the three species of mountain viscacha, the Peruvian lives the farthest north. Like all mountain viscachas, this species prospers in large family groups, or "viscacheras." Typically a viscachera is made up of several smaller family groups. Each family occupies its own cave or crevice within the colony's territory. For most of the year, these are very happy families. Quarrels occur only during the spring breeding season (October through November). When they are ready to mate, the adults become quite irritable.

Although their fur is not as highly prized as that of the chinchilla, mountain viscachas have been overhunted. Their pelts became especially valuable after hunters killed most of South America's wild chinchillas. Today, the availability of farm-reared chinchillas has helped allow the rebuilding of wild populations of both chinchillas and viscachas.

Red-Backed Vole
Clethrionomys glareolus

Length of the Body: 3¼ to 5½ inches
Length of the Tail: 1½ to 3¾ inches
Diet: stems, leaves, fruits, seeds, and insects

Weight: ¾ to 1½ ounces
Number of Young: 1 to 10
Home: Europe and Central Asia
Order: Rodents
Family: Burrowing rodents

 Forests and Mountains

 Mammals

© STEVE AUSTIN / PAPILIO / CORBIS

If you brush away the leaves on the floor of a European forest, you may find a small highway of tiny paths. The red-backed vole, named for its rust-colored fur, is a trailblazer. It builds a network of crisscrossing paths in the forest soil. To escape the notice of predators, the vole makes sure its trails are hidden under wet leaves and rotting wood. The vole has good reason to hide. Its many enemies include wild cats, marten, and ermines.

The paths of the red-backed vole eventually lead to its round, mossy nest. Most red-backed voles nest in an underground chamber just below the ground or under a rotting log. Some nests can be found as far as 18 inches underground, and a few are high above the forest floor.

Compared with other burrowing voles, red-backed voles are at home in the treetops. Some sleep in warbler nests and even birdhouses.

Red-backed voles begin breeding in early spring. By winter an adult female may have had two or three litters. The daughters that are born in spring are ready to have their own babies by autumn. Each newborn weighs a mere half ounce. It is born blind, deaf, and toothless. When it is about four weeks old, the young vole is old enough to leave the nest and find its own food. Red-backed voles are very busy creatures that search for food day and night. They must get plump before winter, when plants and insects become scarce.

Egyptian Vulture
Neophron percnopterus

Length: 23 to 27 inches
Weight: about 4½ pounds
Diet: carcasses, garbage, insects, and eggs
Number of Eggs: 1 or 2

Home: southern Europe, Asia, and Africa
Order: Birds of prey
Family: Hawks and their relatives

  Grasslands

Birds

© W. PERRY CONWAY / CORBIS

The Egyptian vulture is one of the smallest of its kind, so it must be content to eat the scraps left after a larger vulture has ravaged a carcass. Egyptian vultures also hunt for large insects and pick through the trash at garbage dumps.

On the plains of Africa, this vulture searches ostrich nests for eggs. With its thin and relatively weak beak, the vulture ordinarily has trouble breaking a huge, thickly shelled egg. So this intelligent bird uses a tool. To smash the ostrich egg, the vulture picks up rocks and drops them on the shell until it breaks!

A high-flying Egyptian vulture looks very much like the familiar white stork of Europe. But up close, it is unmistakably vulturelike. Bare yellow skin covers its face. Its head and neck are a shaggy mop of tousled white feathers. The vulture's body feathers are a dingy white, while the tips of its wings are pitch-black.

Egyptian vultures court by swooping and diving through the air. After mating, the pair build a simple nest in the crevice of a cliff or building. Both parents tend the nest. The female often lays two eggs. But because parents do not offer food directly to a particular nestling, the strongest and most aggressive chick is the more likely to survive.

European Black Vulture
Aegypius monachus

Length: 38 to 41 inches
Diet: carcasses and small animals
Number of Eggs: 1 or 2

Home: Eurasia
Order: Birds of prey
Family: Old World vultures, buzzards, and their relatives

Forests and Mountains

Birds

© DENIS-HUOT / BIOS / PETER ARNOLD, INC.

?
Endangered Animals

The European black vulture is the largest of all the vultures. It is a heavy but majestic bird that launches itself into the air with strong, deep wingbeats. Once in the sky, it soars effortlessly, with only an occasional flap of its immense wings. The European black vulture can glide for hours, riding high on currents of warm, upward-flowing air.

When the black vulture spots a large, dead animal on the ground, it swoops overhead to take a closer look and then lands. The black vulture uses its long, powerful beak to tear large chunks of meat and skin from the dead animal's bones. To warn away intruders, the black vulture lowers its head and raises its tail and neck feathers. If its warning is ignored, the vulture may leap forward, striking with its sharply taloned feet. It can inflict serious injury.

Despite its power and aggressiveness, the black vulture population is declining. Fewer than 900 pairs survive today. These majestic birds are threatened by the destruction of their natural habitat. Even worse, ranchers kill many black vultures when the humans put out poisoned carcasses for wolves and other predators.

Before breeding, black vultures perform breathtaking courtship flights. The pair swoops and sails in huge circles high above the trees or at the top of cliffs. After mating, the male and female work together to build a large nest of sturdy sticks.

Griffon Vulture
Gyps fulvus

Length: 3¼ feet
Wingspan: 8½ to 9 feet
Weight: 13 to 20 pounds
Home: Mediterranean region and Turkey east through northern India

Diet: large dead animals
Number of Eggs: 1
Order: Birds of prey
Family: Old World vultures, buzzards, and relatives

 Forests and Mountains

 Birds

© ALBERTO NARDI / NHPA

? Endangered Animals

The griffon vulture can be found on the cliffs of mountains near the Mediterranean Sea and as far east as India. Once hunted and poisoned to near extinction, this scavenger served a very useful purpose. Vultures ate dead cattle that mountain herders left behind. By doing this, the bird stopped the spread of animal diseases. Today the griffon vulture is protected, and attempts to reintroduce it into the mountains have been successful.

This bird uses rising hot-air currents, common in the mountains, to soar high overhead. This master of the air locates its food while flying. After watching an area for several days, it spots the remains of an animal and quickly lands. It stands aggressively over the carcass with its neck stretched and its wings open. This scares away ravens, Egyptian vultures, and other griffon vultures that come in great numbers to try to share its food. It makes loud, high-pitched sounds while it eats. When the vulture is full, it slowly takes off, leaving behind the meat that is stuck to the bones for other birds to pick clean.

Griffon vultures do not mate until they are four or five years old. They build their nests in the shelter of rocky overhangs on cliffs. A female usually lays only one egg. The chick takes its first flight when it is four months old. Adult griffon vultures have dark gray feathers everywhere but on their head and neck. These spots are bare so that they can dig into dead animals without soiling their feathers.

Eastern Wapiti
Cervus elephus canadensis

Length of the Body: up to 8⅓ feet

Length of the Tail: up to 8¾ inches

Diet: grasses, herbs, and woody plants

Weight: up to 650 pounds

Number of Young: 1

Home: Manitoba, Canada

Order: Even-toed hoofed mammals

Family: Deer

 Forests and Mountains

 Mammals

© BRIGITTE MARCON / BIOS / PETER ARNOLD, INC.

The eastern wapiti is the largest of the North American wapiti. Size is important in the wilds of Manitoba, where predators include wolves. The name *wapiti* is a Shawnee Indian word that means "white deer." This descriptive name refers to the wapiti of the Rocky Mountains, which are often pale on their sides. Early white settlers mistakenly called this large deer an "elk," which is the word that the British use for moose.

Actually, wapiti belong to the same species as the red deer of Europe and Asia. North American wapiti descended from red deer that crossed over the frozen Bering Strait from Siberia to Alaska about 10,000 years ago. The eastern wapiti is one of about 12 subspecies, or races, of this wide-ranging species. A subspecies of smaller wapiti lives on Vancouver Island, off the coast of British Columbia, and in Washington, Oregon, and northern California. As mentioned, there is yet another subspecies of light-colored wapiti living in the Rocky Mountains.

Generally wapiti stags, or adult males, gather in herds separate from females and their young. During the day, small groups hide in woods, while larger ones stand in open prairie. Although eastern wapiti are large and heavy, they can move quickly and quietly. They are also good swimmers. Always on the lookout, wapiti run away at the first sign of danger. In fall the stags are territorial and aggressive. The strongest males mate with several does, which give birth the following spring.

Garden Warbler
Sylvia borin

Length: about 5½ inches
Weight: about ½ ounce
Diet: insects
Method of Reproduction: egg layer

Home: *Summer:* Eurasia
 Winter: Africa
Order: Perching birds
Family: Old World warblers

 Cities, Towns, and Farms

 Birds

Summer
Winter

© JOHN HAWKINS / FRANK LANE PICTURE AGENCY / CORBIS

Aside from its bluish legs, the garden warbler is drab brown and looks similar to a dozen other European warblers. However, this species is easily recognized—and much loved—for its sweet, mellow voice. A garden warbler's song, though quiet, is full of long, rich notes.

A small, very active bird, the garden warbler flutters through the underbrush in thick woods, parks, and overgrown yards. It spends lots of time in bramble patches and on low branches. These are good places to find tasty insects. Bushes and brambles are the bird's favorite nesting sites as well. Unfortunately, this leaves its eggs and chicks vulnerable to many enemies, including dogs and cats. As protection the warbler keeps its nest out of reach in the thickest part of a tangled or thorny hedge.

Just as North American warblers winter in the rain forests of South America, European warblers winter in tropical Africa. When garden warblers start their journey southward, they begin by flying southwest to Spain and then turn due south for Africa.

Scientists, long fascinated by the way birds navigate, believe that the garden warbler uses an internal compass and timer to navigate. As evidence, garden warblers who have been put in indoor cages face southwest at the beginning of their normal migration. Then, about the time they would normally reach Spain, the birds turn in their cages and try to flutter south.

Reed Warbler
Acrocephalus scirpaceus

Length: 5 inches
Home: Europe, northern and central Africa, and Central Asia to the Himalayas

Wingspan: 5 inches
Diet: insects and fruits
Order: Perching birds
Family: Old World warblers

 Fresh Water

 Birds

© GEORGE MCCARTHY / CORBIS

The dull-colored warblers of Europe are loved for their melodious songs. The reed warbler is one of the most tireless of these famous songbirds. It trills and warbles day and night, mixing its own call—a repeated "chirruc-chirruc, jag-jag-jag"—with the melodies of other birds.

The reed warbler is one of several similar species that make their home in European marshes and swamps. Its favorite nesting site is among the reedbeds of lakes and rivers. The reed warbler's greatest competitor is the *great* reed warbler, *A. arundinaceus.* More than 7 inches long, the great reed warbler usually takes the best nesting and feeding sites for itself. To avoid the competition, "ordinary" reed warblers often leave the marshes to nest in farm fields.

After mating, male and female reed warblers stay together as a couple. As her mate supervises, the female weaves a deep, cup-shaped basket, which hangs between two or more strong reeds. Unfortunately, reed warbler nests often attract cuckoo birds. Instead of raising her own chicks, the female cuckoo lays her eggs into the nests of other birds. If the reed warbler recognizes the cuckoo eggs, it may toss the eggs overboard or abandon its nest entirely. But the eggs of some cuckoos look very similar to the reed warbler's eggs. If the warblers allow the cuckoo eggs to hatch in their nest, the foreign chicks will push all the other eggs and chicks out of the nest.

Common Oak Gall Wasp
Cynips quercusfolii

Length: 1/16 to 1/8 inch
Diet: plant tissues
Method of Reproduction: egg layer

Home: North America, from southern Ontario to Virginia
Order: Wasps, ants, and bees
Family: Gall wasps

Cities, Towns, and Farms

Arthropods

© HANS PFLETSCHINGER / PETER ARNOLD, INC.

The common oak gall wasp, a glossy black or brown insect, reproduces in a fascinating and complex way. The unusual feature of this insect is that every other generation is all female. The members of this "all-girl" generation do not need to be fertilized in order to produce eggs. Their eggs hatch into both male and female larvae, which mature into adult wasps and then mate. The mated females then produce only female offspring, and the cycle repeats itself.

When she is ready to lay her eggs, the female oak gall wasp places them under the surface of an oak leaf. She injects powerful chemicals into the leaf. These chemicals irritate the plant and cause it to produce a large bump called a *gall*. Some people call the galls "oak apples," because they look like small, dark red fruit. Each gall is filled with spongy plant tissue. At the center of this tissue is a hard, seedlike chamber containing the eggs. More than a shelter for the eggs, the gall tissue is especially nutritious food.

The galls do not harm the trees on which they are made. On the contrary, the work done by the wasps can even be useful. In Missouri, some farmers use oak galls as nutritious food for hogs, cattle, sheep, and chickens. The galls also provide food and shelter for other insects. The oak gall wasp larvae themselves are often eaten by parasitic wasps and ants.

Ichneumon Wasp

Rhyssa sp.

Length: up to 1½ inches
Diet: larval insects (wasp larvae)
Method of Reproduction: egg layer

Home: North America, Europe, and northern Asia
Order: Wasps, ants, and bees
Family: Ichneumons

Forests and Mountains

Arthropods

© KONRAD WOTHE / MINDEN PICTURES

Ichneumons are dark, slender wasps with long, rusty-red legs. The female is unmistakable with her long ovipositor, or egg-laying organ. This ovipositor looks like a dangerous stinger at the end of the ichneumon's slender body. Some species do use it to sting when handled, but the main functions of the ovipositor are to bore through wood and to lay eggs.

Ichneumons are parasitic wasps. The female bores into a tree to lay her eggs on insect larvae that live inside the wood. Sometimes the ichneumon must drill her ovipositor more than two inches through solid wood. The job may take up to an hour to complete.

When the ichneumon's eggs hatch, the newborn feast on the soft bodies of the insect larvae. In doing so, the wasps kill a wide variety of destructive wood-boring and crop-eating pests. The European ichneumon, *R. persuasoria*, also called the "pipe cleaner" wasp, parasitizes the larvae of horntail beetles. The North American ichneumon, *R. lineolata*, lays its eggs on sawfly and wood-beetle larvae.

In parts of the United States and Canada, these beneficial ichneumon wasps are successfully used to control insect pests. This type of pest control, called biological control, is a promising substitute for toxic chemical pesticides—it is beneficial for the environment and for the farmer.

Potter Wasp
Eumenes sp.

Method of Reproduction: egg layer
Home: southern Canada, eastern United States, Europe, northern Africa, and Middle East

Length: up to ¾ inch
Diet: caterpillars and beetle larvae (larva)
Order: Wasps, ants, and bees
Family: Vespid wasps

Cities, Towns, and Farms

Arthropods

© ANTHONY BANNISTER / NHPA

Potter wasps are named for the unique nest they build for their young. By plastering together bits of mud, each female constructs a little clay pot. She hangs her eggs inside the pot, attaching them to the top and sides with slender threads. Then she flies off in search of moth caterpillars and beetle larvae. The potter wasp paralyzes the plump larvae with her sting and then brings them back alive to her pot. In this way, she fills the nest with plentiful amounts of food before sealing it shut. When her larvae hatch, they have an immediate supply of fresh food to eat.

When disturbed, female potter wasps can sting people and pets. Each sting produces a red, painful bump. Yet this is a beneficial wasp because it kills the larvae of many insect pests.

Like other vespid wasps, the potter wasp has long, narrow wings, which it folds against its sides when resting. Some species of potter wasp have shiny purple markings on their dark wings. The potter wasp's body is black with yellow or white markings.

Some species of the potter wasp are very widespread and common in both Europe and North America. Unlike many vespid wasps, the "potter" is not social. Adults associate with one another only when it is time to mate.

Lesser Weever
Trachinus vipera

Length: up to 8 inches
Diet: small fish and crustaceans
Method of Reproduction: egg layer

Depth: 3 to 500 feet
Home: coastal waters off Europe and North Africa
Order: Perchlike fishes
Family: True weevers

 Oceans and Shores

 Fish

© TOM MCHUGH / PHOTO RESEARCHERS

The lesser weever is small but dangerous. It has sharp spines on its cheeks and on the small black fins that protrude from its neck. These spines have grooves that carry poison from the weever's body to the sharp tips. The lesser weever's poison destroys red blood cells and affects the nervous system of its victim. If you should step on one, your foot would swell and become very painful. You would need to see a doctor for an antidote, and even then it might take months to recover from the sting.

Many tourists along the Mediterranean Sea and the European seashore have had the misfortune of stepping on a lesser weever. Unfortunately, this dangerous fish likes to live near sandy beaches—just the sort of place where people vacation. To make matters worse, lesser weevers are poor swimmers, spending their days in very shallow water, buried in the sand with only their eyes and back spines protruding. This is a good way to hide from predators. But pity the poor beachcomber who wanders down the sand barefoot!

Not everyone dreads the lesser weever. Many people think the fish is delicious. Fishermen catch it in nets that they drag behind their boats. Of course, they have to be very careful taking this fish out of the net. Lesser weevers can also deliver a nasty sting to the hand!

European Wigeon
Anas penelope

Length: about 18 inches
Weight: about 1½ pounds
Diet: aquatic plants, mollusks, insects, and other aquatic invertebrates
Number of Eggs: up to 10

Home: Europe, Asia, and northern Africa
Order: Ducks and screamers
Family: Swans, geese, and ducks

 Fresh Water

 Birds

© ERIC AND DAVID HOSKING / CORBIS

The wigeon is one of Europe's best-loved ducks. The handsome male is recognized by his rusty-red neck and head, and by the bright yellow stripe down the middle of his forehead. His plump breast is a soft pink. The female is a bit smaller and considerably less colorful. Her feathers are reddish brown with a white patch on each shoulder. Both have a bluish-gray bill.

The European wigeon is a typical dabbling duck. To obtain food, it tilts its body forward and dips its head under the surface of the water. While floating, the wigeon also grazes on water plants at the surface and along the shore. It is at home in ponds and lakes, as well as in the ocean. Small flocks living at the coast fly to water in the morning and spend the day floating just beyond the shore. At nightfall the group returns to dry land to roost. European wigeons often settle on mudflats, where they search for insects and worms.

The male's call sounds like a high-pitched whistle: "whee-ooo"; the female purrs in a low voice. They mate in spring and hide their nest in tall grasses or reeds. The female incubates the eggs. Her mate stays nearby for about two weeks, guarding the female and bringing her food. He flies off shortly before the eggs hatch, leaving the female to raise their ducklings alone. If her young are threatened, she will pretend to be injured and try to lure the intruder away.

Red Wolf
Canis rufus

Length: 55 to 65 inches
Height at the Shoulder: 15 to 16 inches
Weight: 40 to 80 pounds
Diet: mainly rabbits, rodents, and birds

Number of Young: 2 to 8
Home: southeastern United States
Order: Carnivores
Family: Dogs

 Grasslands

 Mammals

© RICH KIRCHNER / PHOTO RESEARCHERS

Endangered Animals

At one time the red wolf, a member of the dog family, was found across the south-central and southeastern parts of the United States. But farmers and ranchers considered the red wolf a threat because it preys on livestock such as young calves, pigs, and chickens. People hunted, trapped, and poisoned red wolves until very few of the animals were left. By 1991, with only 35 red wolves living in the wild, the red wolf was considered the world's most-endangered wild dog.

Zoos are trying to save the species with captive-breeding programs. In zoos, captured red wolves give birth in a protected environment. Their babies, or pups, have a good chance of surviving. When the pups become adults, some of them are returned to their natural habitats—prairies, marshes, bayous, and forests. Unfortunately, these wild areas are shrinking as people turn forests into farms, prairies into housing developments, and so on. The red wolf's chances for a comeback are not very good.

Despite its name, the red wolf comes in a wide range of colors: not only red, but also brown, gray, black, and yellow. The females give birth to their young in dens, which are located in hollow trees or in riverbanks. The females may dig these dens, or they may use holes made by other animals. During the first few months, the cubs stay close to their den. As they grow, they become more adventurous and begin to explore areas outside their immediate home.

Atlantic Wolffish
Anarhichas lupus

Length: up to 5 feet
Diet: crabs, sea urchins, starfish, and mollusks
Method of Reproduction: egg layer

Weight: up to 40 pounds
Home: northern Atlantic Ocean
Order: Perchlike fishes
Family: Wolffishes

 Oceans and Shores

 Fish

© FRED BAVENDAM / MINDEN PICTURES

The Atlantic wolffish is named for its massive jaws and wolflike fangs. When hauled from the water, it snaps violently. So with its sharp teeth and a good aim, it can inflict serious wounds. According to reports, a wolffish once attacked waders in the rocky tidal pools of Eastport, Maine. But this was unusual. Wolffish generally stay on the rocky bottom of the seabed, well beyond the low-tide line.

In addition to its sharp fangs, the wolffish's mouth is filled with crushing molars. It also has a scattering of small teeth in its throat. This predator's savage appearance is accentuated by small eyes and a rounded snout.

The Atlantic species is distinguished from other wolffish by the 9 to 12 dark crossbars on the body. Its color is dull, but can change depending on the creature's environment. When swimming near red algae, the wolffish turns purplish brown. On clean sand, it fades to an olive-gray.

Atlantic wolffish are often caught in nets set out for cod near Newfoundland, where water temperatures hover just below freezing. They are not caught commercially in great numbers, but are known for their tasty meat. In local markets the wolffish is sometimes sold as "ocean catfish." Its tough, scaleless skin can be made into a fine leather.

Wolverine
Gulo gulo

Length: 2¼ to 3½ feet
Length of the Tail: 7 to 9 inches
Weight: 22 to 44 pounds
Diet: rodents, squirrels, porcupines, beavers, and other animals

Number of Young: 2 to 4
Home: North America, Europe, and Asia
Order: Carnivores
Family: Weasels, badgers, skunks, and otters

 Forests and Mountains

 Mammals

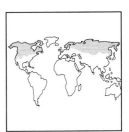

© D. ROBERT & LORRI FRANZ / CORBIS

Wolverines are the largest members of the weasel family. They look like small bears. Their blackish-brown fur is long, glossy, and water-repellent. Wolverines are extremely strong and are known to be fierce fighters. Hunting occurs at any time of the day or night, mainly on the ground.

Wolverines will attack and kill deer and other animals larger than themselves. Certainly not bashful, they are strong enough to drag away carcasses several times their own weight. However, wolverines are more likely to attack smaller prey. They even snack on grasshoppers. But the wolverines' favorite food is carrion (dead, rotting meat), and they will do almost anything to get it, including driving cougars and bears from their kills and robbing hunters' traps. They are good climbers and often store food in trees for use at a later time.

Some people use another name for the wolverine. They call it the glutton. A glutton is a greedy creature (or person) with an enormous appetite. Actually, wolverines are no more gluttonous than many other animals that will eat as much as they can when food is plentiful.

Wolverines were once much more common than they are today. Excessive killing by people has caused wolverines to disappear from many parts of their range. Today these creatures are found only in remote areas of cold northern forests.

Woodlark
Lullula arborea

Length: 5½ inches
Home: Europe, Asia, and northern Africa
Diet: insects and some seeds

Number of Eggs: 3 to 5
Order: Perching birds
Family: Larks

 Cities, Towns, and Farms

Birds

© ALAN WILLIAMS / NHPA

Have you ever heard the expression "happy as a lark?" It comes from the joyous sounds made by species such as the woodlark. Woodlarks are most melodious in early spring, when they migrate from the area around the Mediterranean Sea to Germany. The males arrive first and try to establish personal territories. They announce their land claims by singing loudly from fence posts and bushes.

The male woodlark courts his mate with a song and a soaring flight. He circles in wide spirals and then plunges recklessly toward the ground with his wings closed, only to swoop upward again at the last second. All the while he sings a lively, fluty tune.

After mating, the female builds a neat, cup-shaped nest out of thin, stringy roots and clumps of moss. When their eggs hatch, both parents keep busy gathering caterpillars, beetles, and flies for their young. The adults return to the nest only after gathering many insects, which they smash together in their short, pointed bill. Each parent then divides its food packet among the hungry, peeping chicks.

Newborn woodlarks mature quickly and are ready to fly as soon as nine days after they hatch. This usually leaves time for the parents to produce a second brood. Sometimes the older brothers and sisters remain near the nest throughout the summer. Then the entire family flies south together.

Green Woodpecker
Picus viridis

Length: 12 to 13 inches
Wingspan: 16 to 17 inches
Weight: about 6 ounces
Diet: mainly ants
Number of Eggs: 5 to 7

Home: Europe and the Middle East
Order: Woodpeckers, toucans, and honeyguides
Family: Woodpeckers

 Cities, Towns, and Farms

 Birds

© JOHN JEFFREY / NHPA

Each spring the loud, ringing laugh of the green woodpecker is heard throughout Europe's parks and gardens. This large bird once preferred life in the deep forest. But long ago, humans cut down most of Europe's vast woodlands. Instead of disappearing with its natural habitat, the green woodpecker adapted to a new one. It moved into parklands, orchards, and gardens. Today green woodpeckers actually avoid the reforested areas that they once called home.

Male and female green woodpeckers have a bright yellow rump and green feathers across their back and wings. The male wears a broad red mustache edged in black and is distinguished by large black eye-patches. The female's mustache is completely black, and her eyespots are much smaller. During its first summer, the young green woodpecker looks quite different from its parents. The chick's speckled black-and-white plumage helps camouflage it from predators.

Green woodpeckers eat mainly ants and ant larvae. During the summer, they lick the ants off the ground and from branches and tree trunks. The bird's long tongue is coated with a sticky saliva that works like flypaper. In winter, when ants retreat from the cold, the green woodpecker must find the ants' nests. The bird scratches the nest open and licks up the ants and larvae inside.

Feather Duster Worm
Spirographis spallanzani

Length: up to 10 inches
Diet: plankton
Method of Reproduction: egg layer

Home: Mediterranean Sea and adjacent Atlantic waters
Order: Sedentary polychaetes
Family: Fan worms

 Oceans and Shores

Other Invertebrates

© CHRISTOPHE MIGEON / BIOS / PETER ARNOLD, INC.

As the sun rises over the Mediterranean Sea, the feather duster worm stretches out its fan of tentacles. Each worm's beautiful fan has a slightly different color pattern, in shades of orange, brown, and white. Along the long, feathery tentacles are rows of countless tiny hairs called cilia. As the cilia whir through the water, they draw floating plankton into the creature's long, sticky tentacles. The cilia then sweep the food down the length of the tentacles and into the worm's mouth.

The mouth and body of the feather duster worm lie inside a papery tube that the creature creates by patching together bits of dead plant and animal matter. The worm catches and sorts these bits of sediment with its tentacles in the same way that it gathers food. If one imagines the tube to be a handle, and the worm's tentacles to be a brush of feathers, the creature's descriptive name is easily understood. At the first sign of danger, a feather duster worm quickly withdraws its tentacles and pulls them inside its tube.

These worms have primitive eyes that sense only light. Thus, they can recognize an enemy—such as a predatory fish—only by detecting its shadow. Flounders have a particular fondness for feather-duster tentacles. Fortunately for the worm, it can usually regrow tentacles that have been attacked and eaten.

Green Fire Worm
Hermodice carunculata

Length: 10 inches
Width: ¼ inch
Diet: corals and sea anemones
Home: coastal waters of the Mediterranean Sea and the western Atlantic Ocean

Method of Reproduction: egg layer
Order: Free-swimming bristle worms
Family: Poisonous bristle worms

  Oceans and Shores

Other Invertebrates

© LAWSON WOOD / CORBIS

If you were to wade in water where the green fire worm lives, you would do well to watch out—this brightly colored creature is armed and dangerous! The fire worm is bright green, with red gills and white bristles. The bristles, which contain poison, break off easily when touched and can quickly enter a person's skin. The poison causes a painful burning sensation.

At first glance, a fire worm looks just about the same from one end or the other. But close examination reveals a definite head on one end, with five short tentacles, two pairs of tiny eyes, and a sharp-jawed mouth. Its body consists of many similar ringlike parts called segments. Each of these segments has a pair of fleshy, paddlelike bulges called parapodia. Each parapodium has gills and bristles. The parapodia are used both for respiration and locomotion. In other words, the green fire worm breathes through its feet!

Green fire worms live from the low-tide line to depths of about 50 feet. They are found on coral reefs, under stones on the ocean floor, and in grassy areas just offshore. They crawl along the seafloor looking for prey and also feed on coral. Green fire worms remove the living coral animals and leave behind the stony "skeleton" part of the coral. Coral on which fire worms have fed has a white, naked appearance.

Orange Fire Worm
Eurythoe complanata

Length: about 6 inches
Diet: mainly coral polyps
Home: coastal waters around Florida, the Caribbean Sea, and the Gulf of Mexico

Method of Reproduction: egg layer
Order: Free-living polychaetes
Family: Sea caterpillars

 Oceans and Shores

 Other Invertebrates

© DAVID W. BEHRENS / LONELY PLANET IMAGES

The orange fire worm is beautiful but dangerous to humans and sea creatures. Its wide yellowish-orange body is bordered by a row of tufted bristles. The bristles contain a poison that causes a very painful skin reaction. When disturbed, the fire worm arches its body toward its attacker. This causes the fire worm's prickly bristles to spring erect. When touched, the prickles break away and puncture a person's skin. The resulting wound is painful and itchy for days.

Divers encounter the orange fire worm in the warm waters around Florida and in the Caribbean Sea. The creature lives under stones and in the crevices of coral reefs. Its flattened shape is accented by the rows of bristles on its sides. Like other bristle worms, this species crawls by moving its many pairs of stubby paddles, called parapodia. On the upper surface of the parapodia are reddish gills, through which the worm breathes.

Orange fire worms are fearsome predators. As they crawl along a reef, they eat the soft bodies of coral animals. Occasionally fire worms attack creatures much larger than themselves. They have even been known to kill sea anemones 10 times their own size!

Fire worms earn their name from their burning sting. But some also produce a "fire light." Near Bermuda the females emit a glow when they are ready to mate.

Slow Worm
Anguis fragilis

Length: 11 to 21 inches
Diet: earthworms, insects, snails, and slugs
Number of Young: 3 to 26

Home: Europe (except Ireland) and western Asia
Order: Lizards and snakes
Family: Anguids

 Cities, Towns, and Farms

Reptiles

The slow worm looks more like a snake than a worm, but it is neither. The slow worm is a legless lizard, or an anguid. Anguids are harmless to humans. In fact, they are very beneficial because they eat garden pests. The slow worm has a special appetite for destructive slugs and snails. The slow worm hunts for its prey beneath stones and in the damp crevices of fallen tree trunks.

This snakelike lizard thrives in and around both gardens and trash dumps. Away from civilization the slow worm's habitat includes grassy meadows and forest edges. There it lives among the damp leaves and rotting branches on the woodland floor.

The slow worm avoids the heat of midday, although it likes to warm itself in the morning and afternoon sun. It is most active at night. But even in the cover of darkness, this shy lizard prefers to stay hidden beneath stones, trash, and leaves.

As its name might suggest, the slow worm is not at all aggressive—except during breeding season. When it is time to compete for a mate, male slow worms are quick to bite one another. After mating, the female keeps her eggs inside her body until they hatch. Newborn slow worms are often yellow or silvery green, with a long racing stripe down their back. As they mature, some females turn a bright coppery red. Most males lose their black stripe and become quite drab.

43

Grevy's Zebra
Equus grevyi

Length of the Body: 10 feet
Length of the Tail: 22 inches
Height at the Shoulder: 5 feet
Weight: 780 to 990 pounds
Diet: grasses

Number of Young: 1
Home: eastern Africa
Order: Odd-toed hoofed animals
Family: Horses

 Grasslands

 Mammals

© JOHN WATKINS / FRANK LANE PICTURE AGENCY / CORBIS

? Endangered Animals

Of the three zebra species, Grevy's zebra is the largest. It has a white coat narrowly patterned with black stripes on the top and sides. Its belly is white. In the past, these beautiful animals were hunted for their unusual coats. Although such hunting is now illegal, the Grevy's zebra still is threatened. People have destroyed much of the zebra's grazing land and prevented the animal from reaching its scarce watering holes. Often the zebras simply die from thirst. In addition to the menace posed by people, Grevy's zebras also must fear natural enemies such as lions and hyenas.

Grevy's zebras are sociable animals that usually live in small herds of up to 14 members. Occasionally they form herds

with another species, the Grant's zebra. They remain segregated by gender, however, with males (stallions) living separately from females (mares) and young zebras (foals). One easy way to tell the Grevy's zebra from other species is by its ears—the Grevy's has larger ears than any other species, and, as a result, its hearing is excellent.

A female zebra is pregnant for more than a year! She gives birth to a single foal, which usually weighs about 90 pounds. The baby zebra is quite strong; it can stand on its own when it is less than an hour old. Within a day or so, the baby is able to keep up with its mother as she travels across the grasslands with the rest of her herd. Grevy's zebras have a life span of 20 years.